Faded thoughts of poetry

Published by Maeker LLC.

Copyright 2022 Maeker LLC.

ISBN: 9798798604913

This book is dedicated to my beautiful
son,

Noble Tharten Bey

I will always love you!

I solemnly promise this, that before I
die
Before anyone gets the chance to cry
I'll leave a big chapter of my life,
What it is you ask?
Well, well, you can't see it with just
any eye
You'll have to look deep within your
heart
To all the times we had
For all the jokes we laughed to
To all the love I have for you
And just don't think goodbye.

If today was yesterday and tomorrow
a dream
When would we have met?
I thought our fates were destined
But that was far from the truth
I tried to fight a harsh reality
But it kept me in a tight clutch
I wish that it was not so
And I hope that you can understand
Years apart a world of difference
I exit you enter
Our paths never meet
Preoccupied in my own environment
That just does not include you
Don't take me to be cruel
These things I do, I don't really mean
I would never go out of my way to
hurt you
Frankly
These words I speak,
Denying you is not my pleasure,
But a misery, I must live with too
If God could grant you one wish
What would you choose?
I give you my word and all that it
entails
that forever will I remember you
so part now, but stay always
And then yesterday was a dream
Tomorrow a mere thought
And today bitter sweet sorrow.

I took my first step
The day I stopped the cries
And then came the answers to
everything I questioned why; Why I
loved him so much
Why I allowed his beatings
Why I could do nothing but cry
Why, I hadn't told noone until it came
to the point that I almost died
Why, I told lies every time I got a
black eye
Most importantly
Why did I stay
And then the answers came
When I left without saying goodbye.

This man I knew had no type of luck
He lost his wife and all of his pride
with it
He would always be hurt, never to go
a day happy
Why I would ask him,
Because I lost my wife
He did not reply
Then why young man?
Until I find the love of my life
I shall not roam free and happy
But when she arrives
This love of my life
Then will appear
The man that no longer cries.

I got tired before I even really began
to go anywhere
I reached a brick wall
And there was no way that I was
getting by
A door would be nice
But there was none in sight
So I turned around and I just went my
own way
There was little point in trying
When the wall seemed relentless on
letting me by
So I may have lost out
But I will never know
Hate to say it
But I officially have given up.

I say I want you,
But my actions lack intensity
I love you,
But most of the time you ask a lot of
me
So I turn the cheek
And try my hardest to swallow my
pride
They say the means justify the end
And I'm waiting for Armageddon
And I lose myself in you,
And I only wish to be a part of you
I wait
No, I long for the day that we will
unite
And become one.

Why do we do it to ourselves?
And then ask him to fix it
There isn't a day that he isn't there
I have nothing left to give
I need him to create in me a new
To know that what that was
Is not the example of love that God
had intended it to be
I wish I didn't only write when my
heart ached
I wish I could write when I was happy
But no one wants to hear that
Only my joy rarely inspires me
It's as if my pen can only recognize
pain and despair
But it's all I have to give in times like
these.

I thought that I was through
And that nothing could bring me back
to you
I look over my shoulder and fear
rushes over me
I clutch to my purse
I walk faster but my speed is not up
to par
I make a sharp turn to catch a breath
After I turn the corner, I look left,
then right
Making certain you have yet caught
me
But I forgot one thing
So as you fell from the sky
Dropping on me like a ton of bricks
I find myself trapped
With no where else to go
You finally got me
Damn now what's left to do
Time to accept my fate
And allow your love to come through.

When you lose, you lose
And you're lost in the pool of your
sorrow
Your head is spinning your tears form
a puddle of water that chokes you in
the worst imaginable way
You try to grip on to life
And just when you thought you had
reached salvation
The weight of it all
Causes you to collapse to the floor
The memories trickle up the back of
your neck
The scars you bear are your constant
reminder of what was
And more you think of what could
have been
When you thought you moved on
He made a complete circle
This pain
Love has come and left my door like a
quiet whisper in the night
If only I knew then what I know now I
would have ignored the door knock
And closed the shades and would
have been safe from harm.

I lack the words to express my joy
But so much is going on inside
I search for the words and they lose
itself on my tongue
I bite my lip head in the air, squint
one eye, and the words are still not
there
I am so excited
I've been waiting for so long, and the
time is finally here
I can truly see it
Everything is right there, nobody gave
you this joy, so cant nobody take it
away
Years and years, and your time is now
Life is so beautiful when it's pure
I've had to endure so much to receive
so little
I try not to look forward, but instead
straight ahead
Look too long and my hopes are lost
Look too fast and my joy is gone
Sigh of relief as I try to reflect on the
moment
Try to focus only on it
And what tomorrow brings in the
future and the present is here and
now.

Fought hard to stand here before you
today
Proud and wise
For our children can walk free in the
streets where the blood of our fathers
who lead us to this great day
Years and years
Battles both silent and loud heard
across the globe
And finally, a day of restoration
where our debts will be paid too
many tears shed
To get to this day, when peace shined
bright to clear the way for a new day
So remember this day, because they
thought of us when they stood strong
that day
Some few years back.

I'm stressed but it's a good stress,
I'm stressed because I want to
succeed
But I know it is not going to come
easy
I got to work extra hard to be my very
best self
Got to maintain my cool
When I feel like I'm under pressure
Got to be, got to be
Echoes in my head
Because I hunger for more
No way out,
Ready, yeah I'm ready
More than I will ever be
I want so much more out of life
I'm willing to make all the sacrifices
I'm ready
Just show me the way to the door.

Life moves fast if you don't keep up it'll
just pass you by
But don't speed, or you'll run a red light
Be careful and look both ways
If you end up at a dead end, back it up a
little, take your time, and then make a U
turn
Make wise decisions while you're on the
road called life,
When you get stuck at a fork
It's okay, whichever way you go,
Understand sometimes accidents can
happen
But be assured, you'll make it
And continue on with your journey
Watch out for others sometimes they can
block you
But keep your stamina
Control your rage
The world is huge so don't get stuck in one
place
Don't settle for less, go out and seek the
best
Don't get too caught up in the fast lane
Or you may break down in the process
Sometimes it's easier to stick to what you
know best,
Explore, enjoy
But remember, it's only one time deal with
a limited warranty.

There's only a moment before we will
meet again
It's only a wall that keeps us from
each other's hand
It only takes your breath to whisper,
and I'll be back again
God took your rib, and you felt all
your life that's something was lost
I came about and you were made
whole again
Count all the stars and its sum isn't
even half of how much I care for you.
You are my sun, and without you I
have no day
You are my ink without you
There is no use for a pen
You are my tissue now dry my tears
Let your love come through loud and
clear.

If diamonds are a girl's best friend
Then you are 20 carat stone
If dogs are a man's best friend, then
I'm your pet hound dog
If logs light the fire that keep me
warm
Then you're a 200 foot pine tree
If right was wrong and wrong was
right with no in between
Then loving you would be treason
If up was down and the world was
actually flat, it would take me a
shorter time to reach you
If your love was a song
Angels would clip their wings to come
to earth to let their ears hear such a
beautiful melody
If these walls could talk they'd tell
you how much I love you
If I could not see I feel my way
towards you
If my lips could not speak
I'd use my hands to sign I love you
If I could not live on this earth, then I
wait the years from Mars to be with
you
If my words don't tell you how much I
love you, than maybe this poem will
do.

From the depths of zion onto the
golden gates of heaven
We roam together as a nation of one
From the cotton fields to our masters
home
We stand not divided but strong as a
nation of one
Over the years of our people
We have come far and long from the
land of our ancestors
To the home of our mother and
father's,
We have arrived through all our Perils
through life
We have survived as a nation of one
Always remember your black pride.

The pride that I can no longer hide,
Which I've always kept deep inside
Was set free today
To let everybody see my special
delight
The joy that I have
The happiness that I share to the
roots from my family
To the roots in my hair
I am proud of who I am, the color of
my skin
Down to the blood that runs through
my veins
I am proud of who I am, you can refer
to it as cockiness, or whatever you
like, but I just wanted to let you
know.

Just as angelic as an angel
Sweeter than the sweetest honeycomb
Smarter than any scientists
As beautiful as a fresh rose as
delicate as a flower
That was she magnificent in every
way
And just a lovely sight to set upon
Voice as soothing as nice warm water
Frame as sturdy as a beast
Swift just like a bird
Yes, that was she
Cunning like a fox
Wise like the owl
Old as a great tree
Yes, that was she,
As she lay to her final resting place
Known as our queen she will always
be in our hearts
Forever close is she.

To my dreams and aspiration, which
will never die
I hold you very dear to my heart,
To my goals in which I would like to
accomplish
I know I will one day achieve each
and everyone of them
To my hopes and fears,
Which can only be dealt with care
Always Near in whatever I may do
They help me get through for every
fear I have conquered
I gain inner being,
And my pride and dignity,
Let's just say, I can never leave home
without you
To all of me
What makes me who I am
I guarantee you will always be
satisfied.

We have mentioned the door
But we have to walk through it,
Like everything else in life you can
either be taught or pick it up along
the way
We have been shown many paths
But we choose the one we will walk
along
We have made many mistakes
But we have done an even greater
amount of good deeds
We have tried many battles,
But for each we have fought to see the
light day.

If you ask me how I would like to die
I would reply
Like an angel playing the harp
Like a fisherman who caught the
catch of the day,
Like a fat man that laughed too hard,
Like a boy who won first prize,
Like a black man, waving his rights,
Like a young woman, regaining her
pride
All of these I could reply
But more simply
I would like to grow old with gray
hairs and then die.

A glim of hope and the thought of
tomorrow
Being better than today keeps me
going
Remembering a better time a
stronger me
The mistakes I have made the lessons
I have learned
Have all shaped me
My imperfections make me flawless
My courage to continue separates me
from the rest
My trust in you alone is my only
motivation
That my circumstance will change
My patience will be your victory
All I have left to do, is give it all to
you,
Because my efforts are the
groundwork for the great things That
you have yet to do.

I ran into love today,
but it did not recognize me
I tried and failed to gain his
attention, but I refused to give up
Then and there, I knew one day,
I will get a second chance
A chance I'll take over and over again
Until that day comes when love
reaches out to me
And I can say at last, that it is me that
you seek,
And not the other way around
Because I have paid my dues
And it'll be time to look love in the
eyes.

My smiles I wear to hide my true
fears
My eyes still cannot hide my true self
The cheers and jeers as I walk the
halls
All their smiles look the same,
Yet are all their hearts the same
Do you like me for my style?
Because once in a while I make you
smile
Or do you like me for my true self?
How can I ever tell when I myself
deny my true self
A poet said it years and centuries
before my time
"To thine own self be true"
But how can I be true when the truth
hurts
But then I think of the greatest artists
of our time
Joy wouldn't feel so good if it wasn't
for pain
But I feel the pain
But seldom feel joy
But I tell myself I'm happy
And I really am
But still, even on the sunniest day a
short storm can appear.

<u>The pain of letting go</u>

So much was given
Time, myself, all this I gave to you
So you must understand why it is so
hard for me to get why you are
leaving
Yes of course your reasons explains it
all
You say that I am too good for you
Yes, silly of me to treat you right
Yes, yes,
Someone like me deserves better
But what is better?
You tell me?
When better for me is being with you
My heartaches and my eyes cry,
My soul screams
Why me? Why me?
I want to say I learned something
I want to say I'll be just fine
I want to forget you, and I try my
hardest to do so
But you did me no wrong
So it makes it hard for me to hate
you, and I really want to
I want to say I wish I never met you,
But I know that's not true
But again I have to give time myself
and that's the pain of letting go.

You place me in this category that I
don't even fit in
You tell me who I am
When you don't even know me
You think you can tell me how I feel
When there is little that I am feeling
You tell me this, you tell me that and
I'm tired of hearing it
I want to shout out to the world
So they would stop harassing me
I just want to be me
It's really not that complicated
If you would just try to understand
me
Maybe one day you will see and
accept me for me
And not something you wish I would
be
This is me try harder to see
Misunderstood I refuse to be.

My Sister

My sister what more words can I say
Woman of wisdom, give me the
strength to see another day
Give me your courage so that I can
carry the weight of sorrow on my
back
My sister, my sister
I beg and plead that you let me walk
in your shoes
Your fine dainty shoes
That have walked the path of least
chosen
Let me wash your hands and head
Your wounds the years and struggles
the battles that you've won my sister
Take my seat I beg of you
Let me sit on the floor beside you so
that I may here the trials you have
overcome
Let me step out today, so you can
finally rest tomorrow
Let me hold the torch and carry it's
flame my sister
My sister your passion is my own and
this is my fait my sister
I so humbly thank you.

Man in the moon

Man in the moon with your great big
eye,
You shine the way, in that great dark
sky,
You help us find our way when we're
lost at night,
Man in moon, whoever you are
Thank you for your light
And your strong might
To stay bright, all through the night.

<u>Dear You</u>

Dear you,
I've had something I have had to say
That has been on my mind for quite a
while now
But it's not exactly what you think
I know, I'm pretty sure you're tired of
hearing that by now
So I thought I'd tell you something
new
You and I; are a great pair
I've realized this was true,
As I open up and let go of my fears
More and more
I'm finding out how much we have in
common,
How much we are alike
But yet still in so many ways different
I think the little bit of difference will
wedge and grow
And somehow keeps us a part.

<u>Amazing we are</u>

How is it that we can come home after a
long day and still nurture our children
How can we, the so called weaker sex
Raise such fine strong and powerful men,
all on our own
And they say they don't need us
Yes, I believe if I will say so myself
Beautiful, intelligent, oh the list is endless
James Brown said it "This is a man's
world"
But ladies wait
He also said it would be nothing without
us
And indeed, it would be empty
We are strong, even when we feel weak
We are a voice that cannot go unheard
We are jewels that should only be
cherished
We are forgivers and the backbone in the
home,
Making sure everything is running right
We are accountants without degrees,
We are teachers beyond the classroom
We are a burst of energy that just never
stop
Yes, yes
Amazing we are.

At times when I feel that I am all alone
Not a friend in the world
I think about her
The little girl I saw the other day on TV
The one that had the puppy dog eyes and dirt
smudges on her face
The one walking with the guy asking us to
donate some money
The one that lives in the slum
But yet still somehow kept the smile on her face
And then I don't feel so alone anymore
And if I do,
I think about the widow mother that lost her
father,
Her brother and husband, on the day the twin
towers collapsed
I think about her fatherless children
I think about the bills piling on
And her lack of experience because she decided
to stay home and raise the children
I think about each individual tear she sheds
Each and every night
She sleeps on a couch because the space in her
bed is too great for her alone
And then I remember that my loneliness is
temporary
Because I'll be home soon
In the arms of my family
And like the man I saw begging on his knees on
the subway
Years of poverty taking its toll
He has reached a breaking point, hoping this
night when he finally finds a peaceful place to
rest. He won't awake and his pain will finally be
gone
I think about a boy whose only dream was to be
an all track star runner
But one day while he was jogging he was hit by a
drunk driver who ran the red light
I think I'm alone, but I'm really not
Think that I'm suffering
But my troubles are small indeed.

As I await absolute certainty
My mind is boggled with a thousand
thoughts
Is this really for real?
We have been blessed and most
importantly fortunate to be chosen
Prayers for a healthy full term
Preparation to transition into this
new role
As ready as one will ever be
For this is a dream fulfilled
Excited and nervous at the same time
Please let this be our time.

Thank You God for keeping my heart
in one piece
So I could be whole for him
Thank you to his parents for raising
this beautiful specimen of man
Thank you Mom for allowing me to be
here and now to reap the benefits of
all that is to come
Thank you sir for allowing me to live
in my fullness as the woman I've
always wanted to be
Thank you time for allowing us to
meet when we did
Thank you to our spirits for finding
peace in each other
Truly thankful to love and be loved
with endless memories to come